WORLD'S GREATEST ATHLETES

Kevin GARNETT

By Ted Keith

The Child's World
www.childsworld.com

Published in the United States of America by The Child's World®
P.O. Box 326 • Chanhassen, MN 55317-0326
800-599-READ • www.childsworld.com

ACKNOWLEDGMENTS

The Child's World®: Mary Berendes, Publishing Director

Produced by Shoreline Publishing Group LLC
President / Editorial Director: James Buckley, Jr.
Designer: Tom Carling, carlingdesign.com
Assistant Editors: Jim Gigliotti, Ellen Labrecque

Photo Credits
Cover: Corbis.
Interior: AP/Wide World: 5, 6, 10, 13, 15, 17, 19, 27, 28; Corbis: 1, 3, 9, 16, 20, 22, 25, 26.

LIBRARY OF CONGRESS
CATALOGING-IN-PUBLICATION DATA

Keith, Ted.
  Kevin Garnett / by Ted Keith.
    p. cm. — (The world's greatest athletes)
  Includes bibliographical references and index.
  ISBN-13: 978-1-59296-790-2 (library bound : alk. paper)
  ISBN-10: 1-59296-790-6 (library bound : alk. paper)
 1. Garnett, Kevin, 1976——Juvenile literature. 2. Basketball players—United States—Biography—Juvenile literature. I. Title. II. Series.

 GV884.G37K45 2007
 796.323092—dc22
 [B]

                                              2006029253

CONTENTS

INTRODUCTION

A Whole New Ballgame 4

CHAPTER 1

High School to the NBA 6

CHAPTER 2

Fast Track to Success 14

CHAPTER 3

A $126-Million-Dollar Man 18

CAREER STATISTICS 29

GLOSSARY 30

FIND OUT MORE 31

INDEX AND ABOUT THE AUTHOR 32

A Whole New Ballgame

WHO IS THE BEST BASKETBALL PLAYER IN HISTORY? Ask anyone and the answer is simple: Michael Jordan. "Air" Jordan led the Chicago Bulls to six NBA titles (1991–93, 1996–98), and was named the NBA MVP five times (1988, '91, '92, '96, '98). He played with grace, power, and artistic ability that are unmatched.

But ask anyone who is the most important player in basketball history, and the answer is more difficult. The **legendary** Wilt Chamberlain was so tall (7' 1") that he forced basketball to change its rules. In the 1980s, the rivalry between Larry Bird of the Boston Celtics and Magic Johnson of the Los Angeles Lakers might have saved the NBA's existence. At a time when the sport was fading in popularity, these two brought fans back to the arenas. And Jordan, of course, with his above-the-rim style, took the NBA to new heights.

Yet even His Airness must step aside. Not even Michael altered the NBA quite like Kevin Garnett, the Minnesota Timberwolves' 30-year-old superstar. In 1995, "KG" was the first player in 20 years to turn pro directly out of high school. A rash of other players soon followed his example. Second, in 1997, Garnett signed what was the biggest sports contract ever at the time. Finally, he changed what it means to be a seven-footer. Most players his size stay in the lane, grab rebounds, and take shots close to the hoop. But KG is a 6' 11" player who can pass like a point guard and who also won three rebounding titles in a row. Back to our original question: Who is the most important player in NBA history? It just might be Kevin Garnett.

Naturally, Kevin can dunk the ball. But he's a big man who does so much more.

Just like when he was a youngster, these days you can almost always find Kevin with the basketball in his hand.

CHAPTER 1

High School to the NBA

THE NBA'S MOST IMPORTANT PLAYER HAD **HUMBLE** beginnings. Kevin Maurice Garnett was born on May 19, 1976 in Mauldin, South Carolina. Although his father lived nearby, he was never a part of Kevin's life. Kevin was raised by his mother, Shirley, and his stepfather, Ernest Irby. From an early age, Kevin's life was consumed by basketball. "All he did was talk about basketball," says Baron Franks, one of his frequent basketball buddies. "And every time you saw him, he had a ball. Sun up, sun down. Up and down the street. All day long."

Kevin spent hours on the playgrounds at Springfield Park near his home, sometimes playing until well after it got dark. He once described his summer routine as follows: "I wake up around 9, I go to the gym, shower, get lunch, do some errands. By then, it's 4:30 p.m. Time to go to the park. I'd stay there until 11."

Kevin started on the varsity team as a freshman at Mauldin High School. By the time he was a junior, he had grown to 6' 10" and was named the state's Mr. Basketball. He averaged 28.5 points and 18.5 rebounds per game his junior season. Kevin looked like he was on the fast path to greatness. But suddenly the road took a wrong turn. In May of 1994, at the end of his junior year, Kevin was arrested after a school fight broke out. He claimed to be an innocent **bystander**. His record was soon cleared after he participated in a program for first-time offenders. Despite putting the fight behind him, Kevin and his family still knew he needed a change. So before his senior year, they moved to Chicago, Illinois, where he enrolled at Farragut Academy. The previous summer, Kevin had met Farragut's coach, William Nelson, at a basketball camp. Nelson offered Kevin a fresh start in Chicago.

The move to Chicago was rough on Kevin and his family. He was used to a more **laid-back** existence in South Carolina with people he knew. In Chicago, his

Kevin was the state's Mr. Basketball in South Carolina in 1994. Just one year later, he was named the state's Mr. Basketball in Illinois.

family lived in a bad neighborhood. Walking to school past the gangs was a constant challenge.

On the court, no one could challenge Garnett. He was named Mr. Basketball in Illinois in 1994–95 after averaging 25.2 points, 17.9 rebounds,

KG remembers what it was like to live and breathe basketball as a kid. Here, he puts on a clinic for youngsters in Japan.

Kevin McHale—then the T-Wolves' general manager and now their coach, too—was certain that Garnett would be a star.

6.7 assists, and 6.5 blocks his senior season. He was heavily recruited by most of the nation's top college basketball programs, but there was one problem: He had not yet passed his college entrance exams. Throughout his senior year, it was whispered that Kevin might skip college and apply for the NBA Draft. Only three players had ever gone directly from high school to the NBA, and none had done it in the previous 20 years. Would Kevin dare to try something so unusual? If he didn't get drafted, he could have a hard time making a career in low-level basketball. He would have no college degree to fall back on. Even if he did get drafted, there was no way of knowing if a kid fresh from high school could handle the rough-and-tumble battles of the NBA.

On May 11, 1995, Kevin took that chance, and declared himself eligible for the NBA Draft. In the weeks leading up to the draft, he worked out in front of dozens of NBA coaches and scouts. Most came away impressed, but none were as knocked over as Kevin McHale, the Minnesota Timberwolves general manager. Without telling anyone, he began **plotting** to draft Kevin.

"He has the running ability and agility of a six-foot two-inch player," said Flip Saunders, who took over as the coach of the T-Wolves early in Kevin's rookie season.

Not everyone, though, was as convinced as McHale and Saunders that Kevin would make it. "The team that drafts him has to be prepared for the possibility that he will fail," said then-Portland general manager Bob Whitsitt at the time. "The odds are he will."

Young Kevin Garnett

▶ Kevin's mother raised her son according to her faith as a Jehovah's Witness. Jehovah's Witnesses are a Christian sect that tries to lead their life in strict accordance with the Bible and does not celebrate holidays such as Thanksgiving or Christmas.

▶ As a boy, Kevin worked several odd jobs, including stints at Burger King, bagging groceries at a store, and cleaning restaurant bathrooms.

▶ Kevin's stepfather would not allow him to have a hoop in the driveway as a boy. Kevin had to travel to the local courts in order to play ball.

▶ Kevin portrayed NBA legend Wilt Chamberlain in the movie *Rebound: The Legend of Earl "The Goat" Manigault.*

On the night of the draft, Kevin was getting dressed when Coach Nelson called him. The coach had good news: Kevin had passed the college entrance exam! But by then Kevin had already made his decision. Just a few hours later, Kevin officially became a pro player when the Timberwolves selected him with the fifth overall selection.

Kevin was just 19 years old during his rookie season with the Timberwolves. He made an immediate impact, though.

CHAPTER 2

Fast Track to Success

ON NOVEMBER 3, 1995, KEVIN PLAYED HIS FIRST NBA game. The Timberwolves lost 95–86 to the Sacramento Kings, but Kevin impressed fans and coaches alike by making all four of his shots. KG would go on to play in all but two of Minnesota's games for the season. By mid-January he was playing so well that veteran Sam Mitchell volunteered to let Kevin take his place in the starting lineup. "The reason was simple," Mitchell told *Sports Illustrated* in 1999. "He was better. It's no shame to say that."

Despite Kevin's success on the court, he still made some rookie mistakes. Garnett once tried to check into a game, but when he took off his warm-up jacket, he had nothing but a T-shirt on underneath. He had to go back to the locker room to get his jersey.

Teammates, fans, and opponents were all impressed with how well Kevin adapted to life as a professional player.

Jersey or no jersey, Kevin always loved to play. On some days, he would head home from a Timberwolves' practice and go to the local high school for pickup games before heading back to the arena for a game that night.

Kevin finished his rookie season averaging 10.4 points and 6.3 rebounds per game. He blocked 131 shots on the season—a new franchise record. Before his sophomore season, he was already being called the team's best player.

"To be that size and do the things he does is just amazing," then-rookie point guard and teammate Stephon Marbury said to *Sports Illustrated* in the fall of 1996. "Like a player at the One-spot [point guard], he has the crossover dribble and is a good ball-handler. Like a Two [shooting guard], he can shoot the jumper. Like the Three [small forward], he defends and guards guys at the wing. Like the Four [power forward], he posts up and bangs with the bigger guys. And like the Five [center], he blocks shots and **outlets** the ball."

Kevin rose to **elite** player status in the league by midseason of his second year. He was named to his first All-Star Game in February

By his second season, Kevin was playing in the NBA All-Star Game.

In His Own Words

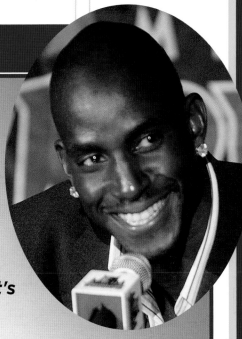

On why KG plays the game (as told to *Sports Illustrated Presents* in the fall of 1996):

"Everybody in this league has to realize why they started playing. It wasn't for money, it wasn't for attention and the crowd. It was for the joy. You got skills, I got skills, let's get started. This is what I do, all I do."

Kevin on dreaming big (as told to *Sports Illustrated for Kids* in March of 2003):

"I've always thought big and always will. You're never supposed to think small because you'll reach something small in a heartbeat."

of 1997. He finished the season averaging 17 points and 8 rebounds per game. It wasn't just his stats that got him noticed. It was also the way he played. When he stepped on the hardwood, he had non-stop enthusiasm and intensity. "I've never seen anyone with his skill level, his enthusiasm, and his size," said his agent, Eric Fleisher, in 1999.

A $126-Million-Dollar Man

AFTER SUCH A **STELLAR** SECOND SEASON, Minnesota knew it had a budding superstar on its hands. For the first time since the T-Wolves joined the NBA in 1989, they felt they had a player around whom to build a championship team. The team called Garnett the "heart of the team and our future."

In late summer of 1997, just before the start of Kevin's third season, the team made every effort to sign Kevin. He would become a **free agent** after the 1997–98 season, and they wanted to lock him in before that. So in August, the T-Wolves offered him a $103.5 million deal over six seasons. NBA great Shaquille O'Neal already had a seven-year, $120 million deal. KG's contract, when it was all said and done, would have paid him slightly more than that.

Kevin was all smiles after signing the biggest contract in NBA history–$126 million for six seasons–in 1997.

"That was our hope," said Minnesota owner Glen Taylor, "that he could say he's got the biggest contract ever and we could conclude this very quickly."

The owner was stunned when Kevin turned down the deal. But Taylor still wanted Kevin above all else, and he was willing to pay for it. Rather than take a chance on having Kevin sign with a different team, he increased his offer. Kevin accepted a six-

KG worked hard to become a force on the defensive side of the ball, too.

year, $126 million contract. It was the biggest contract in NBA history.

The deal was also a wake-up call to the league's owners that salaries were spiraling out of control. Players were getting paid too much money. They felt that the future of the NBA was at stake. So after the 1997–98 season (in which Kevin again made the All-Star team), the owners **locked out** the players. There would be no NBA games until a new contract was signed between the players and the owners. The owners hoped to help reduce player salaries in the future. By Christmas, the league still hadn't started play. But just after New Year's 1999, a new agreement was reached. Under the new deal, the most Kevin could have signed for would have been $71 million. But he had already signed, so the big money was his.

Throughout the lockout, it was still clear to everybody in the NBA that Kevin was going to be a top player for years to come. His mega-contract, combined with his increasing skill level, announced to the world that Kevin made the right decision in skipping college. In the three seasons since he had been in the league, he improved tremendously. He had a fierce desire to win, a stronger desire to get better, and an even stronger desire to make his teammates better. He competed so hard at practice that he made it difficult for coaches to simply teach new plays to other players.

Kevin's hard work paid off. He evolved into the most complete player in the league. Beginning in the 1999–2000 season, Kevin began a streak of six seasons in a row where he averaged more than 20 points, 10 rebounds, and 5 assists per game. No player in NBA history had ever done that before. In the same period, he was named to the league's All-Defensive team each year. In 2000, he helped lead the United States to an Olympic gold medal in men's basketball during the Summer Games in Sydney, Australia.

"It was Kevin's all-around game that impressed

> For six consecutive seasons starting in 1999–2000, Kevin averaged more than 20 points, 10 rebounds, and 5 assists per game.

me, the things you don't see unless you play with somebody," former teammate Latrell Sprewell told *Sports Illustrated* in 2004. "He can post, he can shoot, he rebounds, he blocks shots, he passes, he runs the floor, he makes free throws. What [other] player in the league does that?"

"Kevin is the best in the league by far," former teammate Sam Cassell also said in 2004 to *Sports Illustrated*. "What I didn't understand was KG's basketball knowledge and awareness. He's a guy who studies the **tendencies** of every single player in the league. Nothing gets past him. You don't see that in a young guy."

Unfortunately for Kevin, his team has never been able to duplicate his success. The Timberwolves are no longer the league doormat they were in Kevin's early seasons. But they have yet to win an NBA title through the 2005–06 season. In fact, from 1997 to 2003, the T-Wolves lost seven playoff series in a row in the first round. For the ultra-competitive Kevin, it's a hard reality to face.

"He's not going to let anybody see it, but I know it hurts him," guard Trenton Hassell once said to the *Minneapolis Star-Tribune*. "He's said things about it, that he can't believe we're going home early. He takes all the pressure because that's the type of player he is."

In the 2003–04 season, Minnesota had the most playoff success of Kevin's pro career. Riding KG's stellar regular-season performance (24.2 points and 13.9 rebounds per game), the Timberwolves finished

In 2000, Kevin played a key role in the U.S. basketball team's gold-medal performance at the Olympic Games.

Even more satisfying than earning league MVP honors (above), Kevin led the T-Wolves to the conference finals in 2003-04.

with the best record in the Western Conference and earned a top seed for the playoffs. Kevin was named the NBA's Most Valuable Player.

In the opening round against the Denver Nuggets, Kevin finally led the team to its first-ever playoff series win, dispatching Denver in five games. Round Two proved to be even tougher. Against the electrifying Sacramento Kings, Minnesota lost the first game and won the second. With the series tied one game apiece, the third match-up was in Sacramento. The game came down to the wire. The T-Wolves had a one-point lead in overtime, and needed a basket. They gave the ball to Kevin, who made a fall-away jumper with 10 seconds remaining. The shot iced the win for Minnesota, 114–113.

The series continued to be neck and neck. The teams tied at three games apiece and it all came down to Game 7. Kevin stepped up big time. He led the T-Wolves to a Game 7 triumph (see box on page 26). The Timberwolves lost in the conference finals to the Los Angeles Lakers, but Kevin had already proved himself on the pressure-packed playoff stage. Unfortunately though, he hasn't had a chance to do it again. In the 2004–05 and 2005–06 seasons, the T-Wolves did not make the playoffs.

Although the frustration of never winning an NBA ring weighs heavy on Kevin, he does not let it affect the type of person he is. "Kevin has a good heart," former teammate Gary Trent said. "He not only is a student of the game, he understands life, and he understands people."

That understanding is one of the reasons why Kevin is always willing to give back to his friends,

> **More than anything, Kevin wants to win an NBA championship. But he does not let his frustration affect the type of person he is.**

Kevin's Big Moment

In the 2004 NBA playoffs, the Minnesota Timberwolves were tied with the Denver Nuggets, three games apiece. It was the Western Conference semifinals, and the series came down to a Game 7. The pressure to carry his team to victory fell on the shoulders

of Kevin Garnett. The game was played on May 19, 2004, Kevin's 28th birthday. The Birthday Boy came through like a champion. He scored 32 points and grabbed 21 rebounds—both game highs. He added five blocked shots, including a critical one with just seconds remaining. His defense on the last play of the game forced a difficult shot from the Kings' Chris Webber, and Webber missed. The final score: Minnesota 83, Sacramento 80.

Minnesota coach Flip Saunders could not praise Kevin enough after the game: "I said today at shoot-around that seventh games a lot of times define who you are, and a lot of times the bigger the game, the bigger the player steps up. There was a lot of pressure on Kevin, and he rose to the occasion. I thought he had a calmness about him. He's never been better."

family, and community. Despite being criticized at the time of his contract for holding out for such big money, he has used a lot of it to help people.

After entering the league, Kevin quickly began providing for friends and family, especially his younger sister Ashley, who moved in with him. In 1999, he won the Midwest Division's Sportsmanship Award. In 2006, he was named the NBA's Citizen of the Year. Through Oprah Winfrey's Angel Network, Kevin donated $1.2 million to the victims of

Kevin and some of his NBA friends, including Kobe Bryant, played a game to benefit hurricane victims in 2005.

Hurricane Katrina. His money helped build 24 new homes for victims.

"Through this project, we are directly helping people who need it the most," Kevin said in November of 2005.

Kevin is a man on a mission: to win an NBA championship.

Just as on the court Kevin continues to grow, he also continues to mature off the court. In the summer of 2004, Kevin married long-time girlfriend Brandi Padilla.

Between his marriage, his charitable contributions, and cementing his status as one of the league's best, Kevin Garnett has become an all-around player and person.

He is a far cry from the uncertain player who stepped onto the national stage nine years earlier. The young man who changed the NBA isn't young anymore. He is all grown up, on a mission for a championship ring.

Kevin Garnett's Career Statistics

BORN: May 19, 1976 **BIRTHPLACE:** Mauldin, South Carolina

HEIGHT: 6-11 **WEIGHT:** 220

DRAFTED: First round (fifth pick), 1995

Season	G-GS	MPG	FG%	3P%	FT%	RPG	APG	SPG	BPG	PPG
1995-96	80-43	28.7	49.1	28.6	70.5	6.3	1.8	1.1	1.6	10.4
1996-97	77-77	38.9	49.9	28.6	75.4	8.0	3.1	1.4	2.1	17.0
1997-98	82-82	39.3	49.1	18.8	73.8	9.6	4.2	1.7	1.8	18.5
1998-99	47-47	37.9	46.0	28.6	70.4	10.4	4.3	1.7	1.8	20.8
1999-00	81-81	40.0	49.7	37.0	76.5	11.8	5.0	1.5	1.6	22.9
2000-01	81-81	39.5	47.7	28.8	76.5	11.4	5.0	1.4	1.8	22.0
2001-02	81-81	39.2	47.0	31.9	80.1	12.1	5.2	1.2	1.6	21.2
2002-03	82-82	40.5	50.2	28.2	75.1	13.4	6.0	1.4	1.6	23.0
2003-04	82-82	39.4	49.9	25.6	79.1	13.9	5.0	1.5	2.2	24.2
2004-05	82-82	38.1	50.2	24.0	81.1	13.5	5.7	1.5	1.4	22.2
2005-06	76-76	38.9	52.6	26.7	81.0	12.7	4.1	1.4	1.4	21.8
12 Years	851-814	38.2	49.3	29.8	77.3	11.2	4.5	1.4	1.7	20.4

LEGEND: G-GS: games played-games started; MPG: minutes played per game; FG%: field-goal shooting percentage; 3P%: three-point shooting percentage; FT%: free-throw shooting percentage; RPG: rebounds per game; APG: assists per game; SPG: steals per game; BPG: blocked shots per game; PPG: points per game.

GLOSSARY

bystander a person who witnessed, but did not actually take part in, a particular event

elite among the finest or best

free agent in sports, a player who is eligible to sign a contract with any team

humble modest in conditions

laid-back calm, easy-going; not hurried

legendary remarkable; extraordinary

locked out would not allow the players to practice or play until the situation was resolved

outlets in basketball, to pass the ball up the court to a teammate running toward the basket

plotting planning, or figuring out a way

stellar excellent; outstanding

tendencies things a player most likely will do in certain situations on the court

BOOKS

Before They Were Stars (NBA Reader)
By John Smallwood
New York, New York: Scholastic, Inc., 2003
Filled with fun photos and stories of NBA players from their childhood and teenage years.

Kevin Garnett: Shake Up the Game
By Mark Stewart
Brookfield, Connecticut: Millbrook Press, 2002
Another look at the Timberwolves' star in a book for young readers.

The Northwest Division (Above the Rim)
By Ted Brock and John Walters
Chanhassen, Minnesota: The Child's World, 2006
A history of the teams and stars in the NBA's Northwest Division, which includes Kevin Garnett and the Minnesota Timberwolves.

WEB SITES

Visit our home page for lots of links about Kevin Garnett and the NBA: www.childsworld.com/links

Note to Parents, Teachers, and Librarians: We routinely check our Web links to make sure they're safe, active sites—so encourage your readers to check them out!

INDEX

All-Defensive team, 21
All-Star Games, 16
All-Star teams, 20

Bird, Larry, 4
Boston Celtics, 4
Bryant, Kobe, 27

career statistics, 29
Cassell, Sam, 22
Chamberlain, Wilt, 4, 12
Chicago Bulls, 4
community work, 9,
    27–28

Denver Nuggets, 24, 26

Farragut Academy, 8
Fleisher, Eric, 17
Franks, Baron, 7
free-agent market, 18

Garnett, Ashley (sister),
    27
Garnett, Kevin Maurice
    "KG"
    as an actor, 12
    growing up, 7–11,
        12
    height, 5, 8
    marriage, 28
    personal views, 17
    religion, 12
    turning pro, 5,
        10–12
Garnett, Shirley
    (mother), 7, 12

Hassell, Trenton, 22–23
Hurricane Katrina, 27,
    28

Illinois, 8–11
Irby, Ernest (stepfather),
    7, 12

Johnson, Magic, 4
Jordan, Michael "Air",
    4–5

lockout, 20–21
Los Angeles Lakers,
    4, 25

Manigault, Earl "The
    Goat", 12
Marbury, Stephon, 16
Mauldin High School, 8
McHale, Kevin, 10, 11
Minnesota Timberwolves
    (T-Wolves)
    drafting Garnett,
        11–12
    Garnett's role on
        the team, 5, 16,
        21, 22
    Garnett's rookie
        season, 13,
        14–16
    playoff
        experiences,
        22–25, 26
Mr. Basketball, 8, 9
Mitchell, Sam, 14

Most Valuable Player
    (MVP), 4, 24

National Basketball
    Association (NBA).
    See also All-Star
    Games; All-Star
    Teams
    championships, 4,
        25, 28
    draft process,
        10–12
    playoffs, 22–25, 26
Nelson, William, 8, 12

O'Neal, Shaquille, 18

Padilla, Brandi (wife), 28

Sacramento Kings, 14,
    24–25, 26
salary issues, 5, 18–20,
    27
Saunders, Flip, 11, 26
South Carolina, 7–8
Sportsmanship Award,
    27
Sprewell, Latrell, 22
Summer Olympic
    Games, 21, 23

Taylor, Glen, 19
Trent, Gary, 25

Webber, Chris, 26
Whitsitt, Bob, 11
Winfrey, Oprah, 27

ABOUT THE AUTHOR

Ted Keith is a writer and reporter for *Sports Illustrated for Kids*. He has written for the magazine about many sports and leagues, including the NBA, the NFL, and Major League Baseball.